D1498122

Deadliest Diseases of All Time

Smallpox

Lawrence
Andrews

Published in 2015 by Cavendish Square Publishing, LLC
243 5th Avenue, Suite 136, New York, NY 10016

CPSIA Compliance Information: Batch #WW15CSQ

All websites were available and accurate when this book was sent to press.

Library of Congress Cataloging-in-Publication Data
Andrews, Lawrence, 1955-
Smallpox / Lawrence Andrews.
    pages cm. — (Deadliest diseases of all time)
Includes index.
ISBN 978-1-50260-084-4 (hardcover) ISBN 978-1-50260-085-1 (ebook)
1. Smallpox—History. 2. Smallpox—Vaccination—History. I. Title.

RC183.1.A53 2015
616.9'12—dc23

2014021295

Editor: Kristen Susienka
Senior Copy Editor: Wendy A. Reynolds
Art Director: Jeffrey Talbot
Senior Designer: Amy Greenan
Senior Production Manager: Jennifer Ryder-Talbot
Production Editor: David McNamara
Photo Researcher: J8 Media

Printed in the United States of America

Contents

COLUMBIA PICTURES
presents
The KILLER THAT STALKED NEW YORK
starring
CHARLES KORVIN - WILLIAM BISHOP

Introduction

When is your next birthday? What do you think you'll be doing in five years?

If you had been born a few centuries earlier, chances are you would never have made it to your next birthday, never mind five years into the future, not with a disease like smallpox in the world.

Forty-five years ago, smallpox was a serious threat to humanity. Every year it killed on average three million people. Imagine the population of Los Angeles, California, dying in one year, from one disease. Fortunately for us, smallpox is no longer a constant threat. After many decades of combatting the disease, humanity has conquered it.

Living in the twenty-first century, it's hard to imagine what life was like under the menace of this disease. In the year 1800, English historian Thomas Macaulay wrote:

This poster advertised *The Killer That Stalked New York* (1950), a movie featuring smallpox as one of its main plot devices.

5

Smallpox was always present, filling the churchyard with corpses, tormenting with constant fear all whom it had not yet stricken, leaving on those whose lives it spared the hideous traces of its power … and making the eyes and cheeks of the betrothed maiden objects of horror to the lover.

Smallpox was everywhere from Boston, London, Berlin, Bombay, to Cairo, and if smallpox didn't kill people, it disfigured them. Smallpox scars, or pox, were bigger and deeper than chicken pox scars, and they covered the whole face. The name "smallpox" came from these scars, and helped in distinguishing smallpox from another disease that was common at the time, syphilis, which was referred to as the "great pox."

Smallpox could strike at any moment, and when it did, it spread very quickly. For example, in 1949, twenty-one-year-old Billie Barber watched as her mother Lillian was carried out of their house and put into the back of a mortician's van. The image would haunt her for decades to come.

Just a few weeks earlier, Lillian Barber had been recovering from an operation in a Texas hospital. During her stay, Lillian caught a disease and unknowingly passed it on to her husband, Virgil, who visited her. Soon after Lillian was sent home, both she and Virgil became sick. A doctor came and diagnosed them with typhus fever.

However, it quickly became clear that the disease was more extreme than originally thought. Small spots soon dotted Virgil and Lillian's skin, and both had high fevers. A second doctor that visited just a few days later refused to enter the room where they were resting. He took one sniff of the place and said, "There's smallpox in there." He was right.

History would remember Lillian Barber as the last person to die in the last known smallpox outbreak in the United States. She had infected eight people, including family, friends, and strangers. If left unmanaged, those eight people could have infected more, causing an epidemic affecting millions. When news of Lillian's case reached the public, thousands lined the streets to be vaccinated. Health officials would eventually use up 50,000 pints of the **vaccine**, indicating just how serious this disease was considered.

How did the disease begin, what made it so deadly, and how was it completely beaten? To answer these questions, we must first understand exactly what smallpox is.

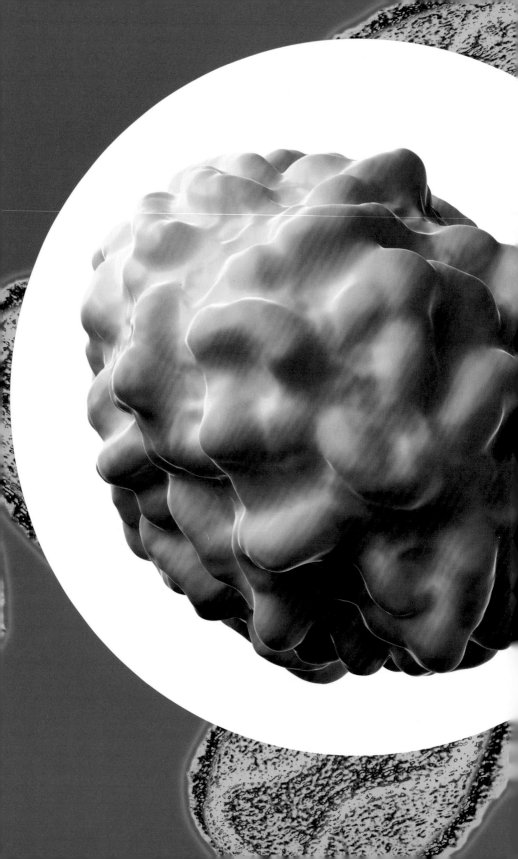

one A Ticking Time Bomb

When you think of a disease, what images come to mind? Do you picture small circular blobs bouncing in your bloodstream? Or maybe you think of a disease as a swarm of invisible wasps attacking your body? Many scientists say the smallpox **virus** is shaped like a hand grenade, brick-shaped and covered in spikes. Like a ticking time bomb, the virus can lie still in your system until the right moment when it explodes.

Viruses are microorganisms that need to live inside the cells of a **host** in order to survive. For smallpox, that host was us, humans. However, there are different versions of the pox in other animals as well. For instance, there's cowpox, horsepox (which died out), sealpox, and insectpox, which melts the insides of caterpillars. Sometimes the pox of other animals can also infect humans.

A computer model of the smallpox virus, which is said to resemble a hand grenade.

You could catch smallpox from an infected person simply by breathing or talking.

Smallpox is much bigger than most viruses. About 300 million of them could fit in the period at the end of this sentence. It can also remain with a person for a long time. Viruses are generally made up of a strand of deoxyribonucleic acid, or DNA, covered by proteins that act as a kind of protective layer. We all have DNA. It's made up of genes, which are the most basic parts of us. In the smallpox virus, there are 100 different proteins protecting a strand of DNA containing 187 genes. Smallpox's complexity continues to fascinate scientists to this day.

Spreading the Disease

Everywhere around the world, every single human being is doing the same thing at this very minute that could have potentially killed them just forty-five years ago, including you. You are not necessarily aware you are doing it, but even if you were, you could not possibly stop, even if you wanted to.

You're breathing.

Smallpox was spread by people breathing it in. It entered the body and found a home in the back of the throat, where it mixed with saliva. Once inside the body, every time someone spoke or took a breath, that person would send little "grenades" of smallpox out into the air in tiny droplets of saliva. The grenades would then stay in the air until someone else breathed them in. This meant that you could become infected with the smallpox virus merely by standing next to someone in a shop or in the street.

Once the virus was in a victim's body, it would start to invade the body's cells. This was a smart virus, and it used the body of its host to help it spread. It would steal bits of the cell's proteins to make a tail for itself, causing it to resemble a microscopic tadpole. The tadpole would then bang into the cell wall in an attempt to escape the cell. At this point, for reasons scientists cannot explain, the cell itself would sprout little tubes that stretched until they touched another cell. The smallpox tadpole would then journey through

A Closer History

1500 BCE Smallpox probably makes the jump from an unknown animal to humans somewhere in the Nile Valley.

250 BCE Smallpox is introduced into China by the Huns.

1438 CE A smallpox epidemic kills 50,000 in Paris, France.

581 Gregory of Tours describes a smallpox epidemic in southern France.

1518 The first epidemic on Hispaniola, probably only a thousand people survived.

c. 1526 Smallpox reaches the Incas in the Andes.

1633 Smallpox strikes the Native American population living near Plymouth Colony, Massachusetts.

1719 Lady Mary Wortley Montagu inoculates her son against smallpox in Constantinople.

1721 *The Sea Horse*, a British ship, brings smallpox to Boston. Nearly 900 people are killed. Cotton Mather begins inoculation in the Americas.

1763 Sir Jeffrey Amherst gives blankets from a smallpox hospital to the Native American population, killing many.

1777 George Washington begins an inoculation program in the Revolutionary army.

1796 Edward Jenner carries out the first vaccination in Berkeley, England.

1800 Dr. Benjamin Waterhouse carries out the first vaccinations in the United States.

1895 Sweden is the first country in the world to be free of smallpox.

1908 An epidemic in Rio de Janeiro kills 6,500 people.

1939 Great Britain is declared free of smallpox.

1958 Viktor Zhadanov, the minister of health from the Soviet Union, calls for an effort to rid the planet of smallpox.

1966 The World Health Organization **(WHO)** announces the Intensified Smallpox Eradication Programme. The aim is to eradicate smallpox in ten years.

1972 South America is declared free of smallpox.

1976 India is declared smallpox free.

1980 On May 8, the WHO declares the world free of smallpox. Humanity has beaten the disease.

1993 The destruction of the last samples of the virus is delayed until 1995.

1999 The destruction is delayed until at least 2002.

2011 Destruction is delayed until 2014.

2014 The vaccine destruction deadline is further extended.

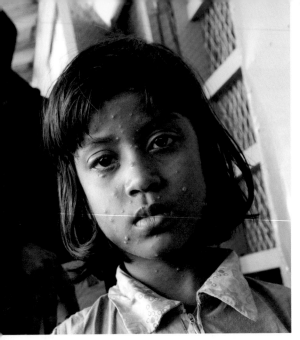
Symptoms of smallpox include many round dots on the skin called "pox."

the tubes and move to a new cell. Since the tadpole moved without actually entering the victim's blood, the **antibodies** in their bloodstream—one of the body's most important defenses—did not know anything was wrong. The virus spread when the first cell exploded and lots of smallpox viruses (without tails) were released. However, even then the antibodies were confused—these new smallpox viruses were covered in armor, which stopped the body's defenses from attacking them. This invasion and explosion pattern continued until the virus had spread all over the victim's body.

The Body Surrenders

You wouldn't notice anything odd until about twelve to fourteen days after breathing in the first virus cells. Then, suddenly, you would start to feel awful, spiking a fever (your temperature could reach 104 degrees Fahrenheit, or 40 degrees Celsius), a headache, and back and muscle pain would begin. What happened next depended on which type of smallpox, major or minor, you had. The minor version killed about 10 percent of the people it infected, most of whom were children. The major version killed between 25 and 40 percent of those it infected (both children and adults).

This next stage would come two to four days later, when suddenly you would be covered in a rash. After another few days, the little spots would grow into blisters, or **pustules**. The blisters would fill with pus, and then after another few days they would dry up, crack, and become scabs. After three to four weeks, the scabs would fall off, leaving you with deep scars. That is, if your body managed to fight off the invaders. If it didn't, then the virus would kill you.

Scientists, even after years of study, are still not sure exactly how smallpox killed people. Most of the time, a victim's lungs stopped working or they had a heart attack. In the most severe cases, however, the virus caused a rash on the victim's skin while it attacked the body's **membranes**, or the sheets of proteins that make up the walls of cells in the eyes, lungs, liver, kidneys, heart, intestines, and reproductive organs. The destruction of these membranes caused the victim's insides to bleed and eventually collapse. Their skin would bleed, turn dark red, or even black. As their body fell apart from the inside, they would suffer horrible pain, and then they would die.

Deadly Contagions

One of the most frightening aspects of the smallpox virus was that it could survive in extreme conditions. It could even remain contagious after a person had died. The virus survived in the scabs on the corpse until a new victim was near, and then it would strike again. If the corpse was put in a place that wasn't too hot or too light, the virus could last inside the scabs for as long as a year.

Some scientists think that the smallpox virus may return as climate change continues to melt the ice in Siberia and Antarctica, revealing bodies once frozen in the earth. Some of these corpses may still have pustules of the virus on their skin, and it's feared that contact with them could spread the virus once more. Though no definite evidence supporting this has arisen, experts are remaining alert.

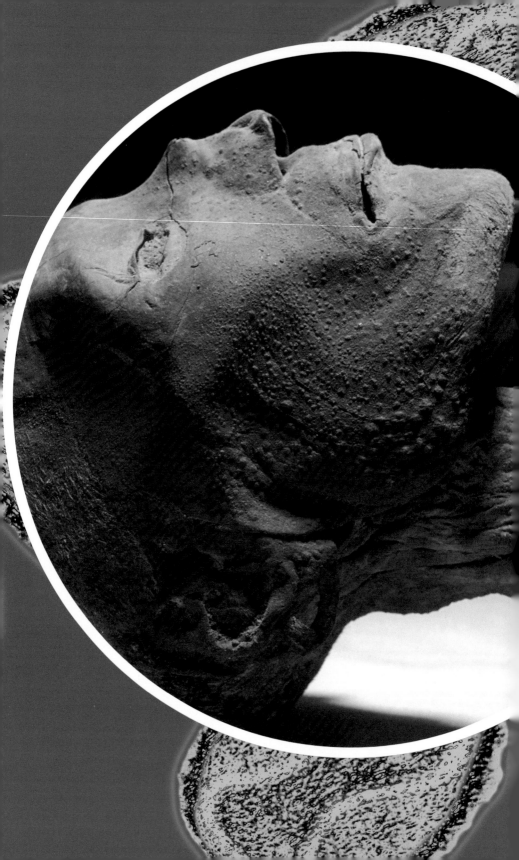

two The Animal Effect

Every major disease that has spread around the world and killed millions of people started in animals. For instance, influenza (or the flu) came from pigs and ducks, tuberculosis and measles from cattle, and malaria from birds. Smallpox also began in animals. Many people who study the history of the disease suspect it first appeared in cows. Around 3,500 years ago, it transferred from animals to humans. This, historians say, would have been around the time when humans were forming farming communities. As more people came into contact with farm animals, such as cattle, goats, sheep, and horses, more opportunities for the spread of diseases arose.

The Dawn of Smallpox

The first case of smallpox in humans probably happened in one of three places: the Nile Valley in

Many people think the ancient Egyptian pharaoh, Ramses V, had smallpox because of the marks found on his skin.

19

Egypt; Mesopotamia, which is an area between the Tigris and Euphrates rivers, now in Iraq; or somewhere in India. One of the first pieces of possible evidence of smallpox comes from Egypt. In 1157 BCE, the pharaoh of Egypt, Ramses V, died at the age of thirty. As was usual for the pharaohs, his body was mummified. When archaeologists found the body and unwrapped it thousands of years later, they found that the pharaoh's face, neck, and arms were covered in large pustules. Scientists say that they cannot be completely sure that Ramses V died of smallpox, but those pustules certainly make it appear so.

Later on, smallpox spread east, most likely through trading. We know that smallpox arrived early in India because Hinduism, the main religion in India, includes a goddess of smallpox. Between 165 and 180 CE, a massive epidemic spread through Rome and its empire. It is believed to have killed between 3.5 and 7 million people, out of a world population of around 200 million, including the Roman emperor, Marcus Aurelius Antoninus. However, the Plague of Antoninus, as historians call it, is problematic. Some historians say it was smallpox, while others say it was measles. In the ninth century, Al-Razi, a doctor in Baghdad, was the first person to note that smallpox and measles were two separate diseases. After his work *A Treatise on Smallpox and Measles* was published, it became easier to identify an epidemic of smallpox.

The Two Versions of Smallpox

Today, experts know that there are two forms of smallpox. The first, **variola major**, is the more severe strain—it causes more deaths and is more likely to leave deep scars on its victims. The second, **variola minor**, causes less scarring and leads to fewer deaths. The word *variola* was first used to describe the disease in 570 CE. It comes from the words *varius* or *varus,* which means "stain" or "marks on the skin" in Latin.

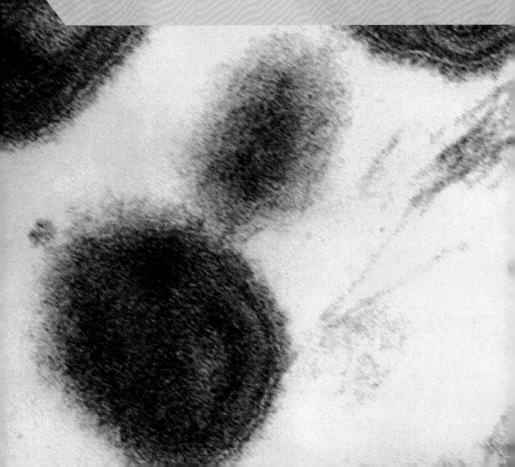

When a disease is common in a society or a community, it is called endemic. The "demic" part of the word comes from *demos*, the Greek word for "people." It means that the disease is native; it lives with the people. On the other hand, when a disease comes and goes, it is called epidemic. *Epi* means "upon" in Greek, so "epidemic" means literally "upon people." It is not native to them or their communities. Don't forget pandemics, either. *Pan* means "all" in Greek, so pandemics are epidemics that don't just stay in one community but move across whole countries or even the whole world, as the flu pandemic of 1918 did.

Smallpox Spreads Further

Between the eleventh and fourteenth centuries, many Christians from Europe went on Crusades to the Holy Land to try to win back Jerusalem from the Muslims. Many crusaders caught smallpox there, and then spread it to populations all over Europe. In 1314, Prince John, a son of Edward II of England, fell ill with smallpox, the disease had spread that far north. He survived, unlike Thadominbya, the king of Burma, who was killed by the disease in 1368.

When Christopher Columbus arrived in what he called Hispaniola, now known as the Dominican Republic and Haiti, in 1492, there were a million Native people living on the island. By 1620, there were none. When the Spanish first arrived on the American continent in 1519, there were approximately 100 million people living in Mexico and Central and South America. By 1620, there were only 1.6 million. How did all of those people die? One reason was that the Spanish forced the Native populations into slavery and stopped them from farming so that they starved. The Spanish also killed thousands outright. However, the diseases they brought with them from Europe, including smallpox, proved to be the greatest killer of all.

In the Americas, there were only five animals the Native people could **domesticate**, the turkey, the llama, the guinea pig, the Muscovy duck, and the dog. When the Europeans arrived, they brought their domesticated cows, horses, sheep, goats, pigs, ducks, and chickens with them. Any viruses these new animals might have carried with them on the boats to the New World now had the chance to jump into the human population of the Americas, with devastating results.

Falling Empires

Smallpox didn't arrive with Columbus on Hispaniola. It took time to appear. From 1492 to the arrival of the virus in 1519, over 300,000 of the Native population had already been murdered or had died from other diseases. For those who had managed to survive, smallpox would be the end. It attacked the population so badly that a Spanish colonialist on the island estimated that only 1,000 Native people were left afterward. As we noted, by 1620 there was not a single one.

VÉRITABLE EXTRAIT DE VIANDE LIEBIG.

LA CONQUÊTE DU MEXIQUE. 2.
Montezuma fait prisonnier par Cortez (14. Nov. 1519).

Hernán Cortés took over Montezuma's Aztec Empire after infecting the Aztec people with smallpox.

Hernán Cortés was a **mercenary** soldier (called a *conquistador* in Spanish). Having heard about a city full of treasure in the middle of what is now Mexico, he decided to find it and see if he could get rich. In 1519, he marched toward the capital of the Aztec Empire, Tenochtitlán. Upon his arrival, he was welcomed as a returning god by the Aztec leader Montezuma, whom Cortés promptly captured. In 1520, Cortés and his troops were forced to return to the coast to stop another group of Spaniards from arriving in the newly found city, and one of Cortés' soldiers became infected with smallpox. When Cortés returned to Tenochtitlán, the Aztecs retaliated against the Spanish, and the conquistador was forced to withdraw with his troops. However, he left smallpox behind. The disease started to kill the Aztecs, and soon a quarter of the population was dead, including the emperor. When Cortés returned, he was easily able to beat the remaining Aztecs. Cortés had finally conquered an empire, but only with the help of smallpox.

The disease then started to spread. It went south, toward the Incas, whose great empire was centered in the Andes Mountains. Smallpox reached them in 1526 and killed their emperor, his heir, and most of the court. This caused a civil war to break out between two brothers fighting to be the next emperor. When a Spanish conquistador, Francisco Pizarro, arrived in 1532, he found the Incas, now led by the victor of this conflict, Atahuallpa, much weakened by smallpox and the war. Pizarro immediately took Atahuallpa prisoner and demanded a ransom of a room full of gold. However, Pizarro did not honor his side of the bargain. He kept the gold, killed Atahuallpa, and yet another empire fell with the help of smallpox.

There were effects on the Native Americans in North America, too. When Hernando de Soto explored the Mississippi Valley in 1540, he found villages and encampments completely deserted, smallpox had arrived there before him. For the most part, however, it cannot be said that the Spanish deliberately introduced the disease, unlike one British soldier.

Cruel Tactics

In 1763, Lord Jeffrey Amherst, the commander of the British forces in North America, wanted to stop Native Americans from attacking his troops. He had an idea and wrote to one of his commanders:

> *Could it not be contrived to send the Small Pox among those disaffected tribes of Indians? We must on this occasion use every stratagem in our power to reduce them.*

A meeting was arranged between the British and tribal chiefs at Fort Pitt near Pittsburgh. The British handed over blankets that had been used by patients in the fort's smallpox hospital. It is not known whether the tactic worked, but it is the first example in history of deliberate biological warfare, or using disease to fight war.

When soldiers were not spreading smallpox across North America, traders and trappers were responsible for bringing it to new places. As late as the nineteenth century, smallpox was coming across virgin populations, as populations with no exposure to a disease are called. In 1837, a steamboat travelling up the Mississippi River from St. Louis encountered the

Mandan, a Great Plains tribe. The boat was carrying two people infected by smallpox. They infected the tribe, and in two weeks 2,000 Mandans were reduced to forty.

If everyone knew that smallpox was such a killer, was anyone doing anything to try to stop it? In fact, people had been trying for many centuries, with mixed results.

Lady Montagu and Inoculation

Lady Mary Wortley Montagu was the wife of the British ambassador to the Sublime Porte, the Ottoman court in Constantinople, which is now called Istanbul. While living in the city in 1717, she heard about a technique that could possibly stop smallpox, **inoculation**. Lady Mary was fascinated by the procedure because she had suffered from the disease as a young woman. She had lost her eyebrows and ended up being heavily scarred, while her brother had died of the disease.

Inoculation was based on the fact that if you had the disease once, you could not get it again. The process was simple: You got someone to give you *variola minor*, you became sick and were **quarantined** until the disease passed, and then you knew you were protected against a more serious strain. What Lady Mary discovered was not a new process. This technique was known all over North Africa, the Middle East, Persia (now Iran), and India. In China, powdered smallpox scabs were blown up a person's nose to inoculate him or her, a technique said to have been introduced by a wandering wise man from India in the eleventh century.

Inoculation was not risk-free, however. There was always the possibility of becoming badly infected. Nonetheless, in 1719, Lady Mary had her six-year-old son inoculated. His arm was scratched, and powdered scab or liquid from a pustule was placed in the wound. He recovered without problems. When Lady Mary got back to England, another smallpox epidemic hit London. This time she decided to have her daughter inoculated. The procedure was carried out successfully and was publicized in the newspapers.

A Royal Treatment

The English royal family also became interested in the technique of inoculation. In 1700, Queen Anne's son and heir had died of smallpox. Caroline, the Princess of Wales, did not want her children to suffer the same fate. However, she insisted that the procedure had to be tested. Six prisoners awaiting execution were given a deal: If they agreed to be inoculated and survived the experiment, they would be allowed to walk free. They agreed, and the inoculations were carried out by Lady Mary's doctor, Charles Maitland, in front of the royal physician, Sir Hans Sloane, and twenty-six others. All the prisoners survived and were released. The royal family still wasn't sure, so they had five orphan boys inoculated.

Caroline, Princess of Wales, was the first in the British royal family to inoculate her children in the early 1700s.

They, too, all survived, and finally Princess Caroline had her two daughters inoculated.

Once the procedure had received the royal seal of approval, it spread across the country and across the Atlantic to the colonies in North America.

The Boston Effect

In 1721, an epidemic broke out in Boston. A clergyman named Cotton Mather, who had heard about inoculation, delivered a sermon calling all doctors in the city to start inoculating people. Only

In 1777, future president George Washington formed an army of soldiers who had survived smallpox.

one, Zabdiel Boylston, was willing to try the procedure. On June 26, 1721, the doctor inoculated Mather's son Thomas and two slaves, Jack and Jackey.

The technique caused a huge scandal in Boston. Some people thought it was against God's wishes, while others thought it ridiculous to deliberately give yourself the disease. Yet Mather kept count, and at the end of the epidemic, six of the 244 inoculated people had died (2.5 percent), while 844 of the 5,980 (or 14 percent) who acquired the disease naturally had died. His figures proved that inoculation was a much safer method of going about things than just letting nature take its course.

These kinds of results caused the procedure to spread outside of Boston—to New York, Philadelphia, and Charleston. It also gained some important supporters, such as Benjamin Franklin and George Washington.

In 1766, smallpox was a major factor in the Americans' loss to the British at Quebec. Washington, who himself had caught smallpox in 1751 and carried its scars, learned his lesson. During the American War of Independence, which began in 1776, he started an inoculation program. On March 12, 1777, he wrote to his commanders:

> *You are hereby required to send me an exact return of your Regiment, and to send those recruits who have had the smallpox to join the Army. Those who have not, are to be sent to Philadelphia, to be inoculated under the direction of the commanding Officer of the City.*

Washington's inoculation program succeeded. With everyone protected against the disease, the army he gathered never suffered from smallpox again, and they were victorious against the British.

However, the procedure still had risks. While most inoculated people suffered from only small amounts of scabs, others were unlucky enough to develop a very dangerous case of the disease, which could leave them disfigured or dead. Also, once someone had the disease in their system, they were contagious. Anyone inoculated had to be quarantined for up to four weeks. This clearly was not the final solution to the problem. The world needed a way to protect itself from the disease without having to contract it. In 1796, that solution arrived.

three The Cow Doctor

How many shots do you think you've had in your life? Ten? Twenty? Thirty? Chances are you've had a lot. Although getting shots may be uncomfortable, without them, you probably wouldn't be here today. How do shots work?

Do you remember those microscopic proteins called antibodies? Well, when something strange enters the cells of your body, the cells react and call in the antibodies. There are different antibodies for different viruses and bacteria. They, along with special **white blood cells**, act as your body's main defense against disease. Their job is to destroy the invader before it can harm you. Antibodies must quickly figure out how to destroy new threats before they can multiply and there are too many to combat.

When you get a shot, it's like giving your body an early warning system. In the case of inoculation, the vaccine **sensitizes** the antibodies so that if they

Today, vaccination is the most popular way of preventing the spread of harmful diseases.

ever meet the invader again, they know exactly what to do—they don't have to work it out.

After the discovery of inoculation came **vaccination**, which sensitizes the body's defenses with a type of virus that is similar to the real target but that doesn't make you really ill. For example, the less-deadly cowpox virus is used as a vaccine against smallpox. The vaccine helps people develop antibodies that make them immune to both diseases.

As a man named Edward Jenner discovered in 1796, a vaccine is like a road map and textbook for an antibody. The vaccine shows it how to get where it's needed and what to do when it gets there. The amazing thing about Jenner's discovery was that he didn't know any of this. He did not know what caused smallpox, how it was spread, or how the body reacted to and protected against disease. He just saw what seemed like a natural way of protecting people, and followed his instincts.

The Inventor of Vaccines

The man who changed the world and its defense against one of the deadliest diseases for humanity was Edward Jenner. He was born on May 17, 1749, in a small village called Berkeley, in Gloucestershire, England. His parents both died when he was five, and his older brother raised him. When he was thirteen, he became an apprentice to a doctor in his hometown. Eight years

Anything for Jenner

In the 1800s, while Britain was at war with France, Edward Jenner's reputation also helped him negotiate several prisoners-of-war releases. The story goes that the French leader, Napoleon, was so impressed by Jenner's vaccine that when Jenner personally wrote to him to ask that he release the men, Napoleon immediately freed them with the words, "Ah, Jenner, we can't refuse that man anything!"

Edward Jenner   Napoleon Bonaparte

later, he went to London to study with a famous doctor named John Hunter. After two years in London, he returned to Berkeley.

He settled down as the local doctor, and in his spare time he studied the habits of cuckoo birds. He was the first person to notice that cuckoos steal the nests of other birds. Smallpox, however, was one subject that particularly fascinated him. He remembered hearing as a child that milkmaids (the women who milked cows before there were machines to do it) often said that they could never get smallpox because they had been infected by cowpox.

Jenner thought about this and decided to try an experiment. In early May 1796, a milkmaid named Sarah Nelmes caught cowpox, and on May 14, Jenner took some of the pus from her blisters. He had found an eight-year-old boy named James Phipps to act as a guinea pig. He made a small wound in James's arm, into which he introduced the cowpox matter he had taken from Sarah. James then developed cowpox. Next came the really important part for Jenner. On July 1, he inoculated James with smallpox. Then he waited.

After the inoculation, James showed no signs of smallpox. The old stories about cowpox protecting against smallpox were true!

Jenner sent his results to the Royal Society, a group in London made up of all the famous scientists of the day. The report he wrote was rejected. Still, he

The version of smallpox that infects cows helped Edward Jenner develop a vaccine for human smallpox.

carried on with the experiments, and in 1798, he wrote another report that he published himself. It was called "An Inquiry into the Causes and Effects of Variolae Vaccinae, a Disease, Discovered in some of the Western Counties of England, particularly Gloucestershire, and known by the Name of Cow Pox." In the report, he called the pus he had taken from Sarah Nelmes "vaccine," which means "from a cow" in Latin. He also called the whole process "vaccination," which is now the word for all shots, even if they don't come from cows.

At first, people were wary of vaccination. It seemed strange to introduce pus from cows into people. Indeed, some eminent doctors opposed to Jenner said that vaccination would turn people into cows! Most people, however, saw that vaccination was a good thing, and Jenner's work quickly started to spread.

There were problems, however. The pus from the cowpox had to be "harvested" at just the right moment or it wouldn't be strong enough. Some doctors mixed cowpox and smallpox itself. Even with these problems, Jenner managed to win over the king and queen, and by 1801, 100,000 people in England had been vaccinated.

There was still one problem remaining—how to produce the vaccine? Cowpox was quite a rare disease, and it could be difficult to find cases. Jenner's idea, which became the leading procedure for years to come, was called the arm-to-arm technique. One person would be vaccinated, and the pus in the cowpox blisters produced would be taken and used to vaccinate the next person.

A World of Vaccination

Eventually, vaccination began to spread around the world. In 1804, a man named Don Francisco Xavier Balmis set out from Spain on a vaccination mission

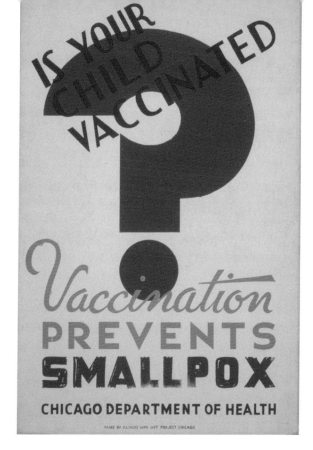

 IS YOUR CHILD VACCINATED?

Vaccination PREVENTS SMALLPOX

CHICAGO DEPARTMENT OF HEALTH

MADE BY ILLINOIS WPA ART PROJECT CHICAGO

Posters like this went up around the United States to encourage people to vaccinate their children.

to the Americas. With him were twenty-two orphan boys, none of whom had ever had smallpox or been vaccinated. One boy was vaccinated just before they left Spain. His blisters were used to vaccinate the next, and so on. The boys were used as a human vaccination chain all the way to the Americas.

There was one problem with this method, and it became one of the arguments used by vaccination's opponents. If the person vaccinated already had a disease, say syphilis, then this disease was passed on with the vaccination. This was solved when Italian scientists started to grow the vaccine directly in cows. Small wounds were made in the sides of cows, cowpox matter was inserted (just like for humans), and blisters were left to grow. Then the blisters were harvested and, sadly, the cows killed.

The success of vaccination also greatly improved armies around the world. Armies were made up of many people staying close together over a long time, and this made them particularly vulnerable to diseases. Vaccination ensured whole armies were protected against the spread of illnesses such as smallpox. In 1805, Napoleon, the leader of France, vaccinated everybody in his army. That same year, doctors in Khiatka, near Russia's border with China, were vaccinating. By 1812, merchants were distributing copies of Jenner's report to people in Samarkand in what is today Uzbekistan. Between 1808 and 1811, 1.7 million people were vaccinated in France, and in Russia, about 2 million people had been vaccinated by 1814.

Vaccination Arrives in the U.S.

In the United States, the technique of vaccination was first spread by a Boston doctor named Benjamin Waterhouse. In July 1800, he received some vaccine from England and immediately used it on four of his children and three of his servants. In May 1801, he sent some vaccine to New York, and a vaccination program was immediately started.

In January 1802, a special center was set up in the city to provide free vaccination to the poor (who were more at risk because they generally lived in crowded and dirty conditions). President Thomas Jefferson became very interested in vaccination, starting programs in Washington D.C., Baltimore, and Philadelphia. He vaccinated eighteen members of his own family, some of his neighbors, and members of Native American tribes.

Vaccination was soon practiced all over the world, and some countries started to demand all citizens receive vaccinations, including parts of Germany in 1807 and Denmark in 1810. Great Britain introduced **compulsory** vaccination against smallpox, and at the same time outlawed inoculation, in 1853. The following year, 400,000 people were vaccinated in Britain.

What had started out as Edward Jenner's experiment on a milkmaid, a boy, and a cow turned into a vital, life-changing scientific discovery that would alter a deadly disease's history forever. However, during his lifetime, Jenner wished for only one outcome for his medical advancement: "the annihilation of the small pox, the most dreadful scourge of the human species, must be the final result of this practice." This dream would not be realized for over a century and a half, but when it was, smallpox, and humanity, would never be the same.

four Humanity Fights Back

While vaccination did reach many people around the world, smallpox still killed millions every year. By the end of the nineteenth century, some countries were making the effort to vaccinate their entire population. In 1895, Sweden became the first country to declare itself smallpox-free. It was soon followed by Puerto Rico in 1899. In the United States, however, smallpox cases appeared year after year. For example, in 1922, 791 people died from the disease. It wasn't long before the U.S. government offered routine vaccination programs to its citizens. These efforts proved successful. Between 1948 and 1965, just one person died from the disease. By 1967, smallpox had been eliminated from North America and Europe. This was not the case in other parts of the world, however, where smallpox killed between 10 and 15 million people each year.

Headquarters for the World Health Organization in Geneva, Switzerland.

The **World Health Organization (WHO)**, founded in 1948, is part of the United Nations and works to improve the general health of the world. It also coordinates attempts to **eradicate** communicable diseases, such as polio and smallpox. In 1958, Viktor Zhadanov, the minister of health from the Soviet Union, spoke at the WHO's annual meeting. He suggested that the world try to eradicate smallpox. Eradicate a disease completely? At first, people were skeptical: How could you vaccinate the whole world? It had never been done before! Just as with vaccination itself, however, the idea slowly took hold.

Tackling the Disease Around the World

The real problem with the idea lay not with the world's determination, but in the equipment it had to work with. The smallpox vaccine had to be used within eighteen hours or it just didn't work. That was fine in the United States or in Europe, where there were lots of modern, well-equipped hospitals. However, half of the world's smallpox cases were happening in India, where travel was more difficult and where there were fewer well-equipped hospitals. This meant that the vaccine was often lost and wasted.

Then a laboratory in London found a new way to make the vaccine cheaply and in a way that allowed it to last for much longer: the freeze-dried vaccine.

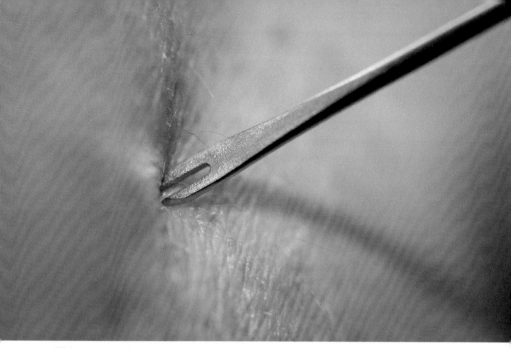

This special fork-shaped needle was created to administer the smallpox vaccine.

Freeze-drying is done by freezing something, then placing it in a vacuum where the ice is sucked out— thus removing all the water. This creates a very stable, portable, storable product. All you need to do is add some water, and the product resumes its previous state. (Instant coffee is freeze-dried, and astronauts eat freeze-dried food in space.) The freeze-dried vaccine made it possible to keep the vaccine for much longer periods without having to worry about it not working.

The next technical achievement was to make a needle that could be easily and quickly used. A new type of needle was soon invented in the United States. It looked like a fork with two prongs, with a piece of wire between them. The right amount of vaccine was held between the two points and the wire. The needle was then jabbed into a person's skin, puncturing it and letting the vaccine enter the small wound. The needle was good because it could be sterilized and reused about 200 times, and somebody with no medical training could use it.

With the new vaccine and needle in place, in 1966, the WHO announced the Intensified Smallpox Eradication Programme. Its aim was to eradicate smallpox from the planet in ten years. (They set the ten-year target after President Kennedy had promised to put a man on the moon within ten years—and succeeded.) An American, D. H. Henderson, was put in charge of the program. At first the idea was to vaccinate everybody on the planet, but as you can imagine, this proved difficult to do, especially in the crowded cities of India and Bangladesh.

A new idea was tried after an outbreak in Nigeria. Over 90 percent of the population had been vaccinated in the country, but smallpox broke out in a religious group that had refused vaccination. The WHO workers were short of vaccine, so instead of simply vaccinating everybody, they decided to find where each new outbreak happened. They would rush to that location and vaccinate everybody in the village. The people with the disease were isolated from everyone else and nobody was allowed to leave the village until the outbreak had died down. While the village was

A Dedicated Life

Ali Maow Maalin was known as the last person to contract the lesser strain of smallpox. Before catching the disease, Maalin had worked as a hospital cook. He had not been vaccinated and because of this caught smallpox. After surviving, his eyes were opened to other diseases facing the world, especially those in his own country of Somalia. He dedicated much of the remainder of his life to eliminating polio around the world. His death in July 2013 was mourned by many, and he is known as one of today's advocates for global disease elimination.

After surviving *variola minor*, Ali Maow Maalin dedicated his life to fighting other deadly diseases, such as polio.

isolated, health workers then went to all the villages nearby to look for anyone with symptoms of the disease. Then they vaccinated those people. This was called the **surveillance-containment strategy**.

The Chain Is Broken

As we have seen, infection works in a chain—one person gets the disease and passes it to more people, who in turn pass it to more people, and so on. If you stop people passing it on to others, you then break the chain. Smallpox was a clever virus, but it had a fatal flaw. It could live only in humans. If everybody was vaccinated or isolated, the virus died out. This surveillance-containment method was very effective in breaking the chain of infection. It soon became the method used all over the world, especially in India, where the smallpox eradication program employed 152,000 Indian health workers and 230 WHO personnel. The program was successful. In 1953, there were 253,322 cases of smallpox in India; by 1975, the number of cases had dropped to 1,436; and by 1976, there was not a single one.

South America was free of the disease by the end of 1972. By the end of 1973, smallpox was found only in the Indian subcontinent and southern and eastern Africa. The WHO kept fighting the disease, systematically eradicating it in all countries until there was just one place left: Bangladesh. On October 16, 1975, a

This is probably the last known vial of the live smallpox virus from India in the 1970s.

three-year-old Bangladeshi girl named Rahima Banu broke out in a rash—she had contracted *variola major*. She was quickly isolated and managed to recover. She also became famous: She was the last person ever to contract that smallpox strain naturally. Two years later, a cook in Somalia named Ali Maow Maalin got *variola minor*. He, too, recovered, and he became the last person to contract the milder form.

Slightly more than ten years had passed since the WHO embarked on their mission. In that time, millions had been vaccinated, until on May 8, 1980, smallpox was officially declared eliminated from the Earth.

five The Virus Today

Although smallpox has been eliminated from humanity, controlled samples of the virus still exist in two places in the world. One place is the Centers for Disease Control and Prevention (CDC) in Atlanta, Georgia. The other is the State Research Center of Virology and Biotechnology (also known as Vector) in Siberia. However, some people worry that those who want to harm populations have obtained large quantities of the virus over the decades. We may never know if that is true, but governments such as the United States are taking steps to prepare for any potential attacks against them.

Keeping the Virus Close

When smallpox was eradicated, everyone agreed that something should be done with the last remaining samples. Some countries destroyed them, while others sent their stocks to Atlanta or Siberia. In 1972, the

The Centers for Disease Control and Prevention are based in Atlanta, Georgia.

Soviet Union (now Russia and other Eastern European countries), the United States, and Great Britain signed the Biological and Toxin Weapons Convention, which banned any further research into biological weapons and promised never to use them. Today, 165 governments around the world have signed the agreement.

However, signing the treaty doesn't necessarily mean obeying the rules. The Soviet Union had started biological weapons research labs decades prior to the agreement. According to Soviet scientists who have relocated to the West, when the Soviet Union collapsed in 1991, many scientists working at the labs left the country because they weren't paid or had lost their jobs. Experts now think that some of them may have taken smallpox samples with them. It is believed that there are a lot more countries holding the smallpox virus than simply the United States and Russia.

On July 1, 2014, a cardboard box containing forgotten vials of smallpox was discovered at a research center in Bethesda, Maryland. These vials were from the 1950s and marked the first time unaccounted-for traces of the virus had been found on U.S. soil. The discovery called into question once again how many other unknown *variola* samples are in the world today.

It has been over thirty years since the last naturally occurring case of smallpox. Most people who were vaccinated will no longer be immune to the disease because their vaccination will have worn out.

Life of the Vaccine

The smallpox vaccine has different lifespans inside the body depending on the person's history with it. For example, a person who receives the vaccine for the first time has immunity for three to five years, according to the CDC. After that, if a person is vaccinated again, they will have a longer immunity. The more the body is exposed to the vaccine, the more likely it is to remember how to combat it and fight it for longer periods of time.

You and many others around the world have never come across smallpox. Our bodies have absolutely no idea what smallpox is. We have become like the Aztecs or the Incas: a virgin population, highly susceptible to unknown diseases.

Making Preparations

Imagine if someone released the virus in New York City. There are over eight million people all crammed together in one place (plus all the suburbs). Say that from that initial release one person gets the disease.

She gets up and gets on the subway to go to work. She passes it to everyone near her. Then she arrives at the office and spreads it to everyone there. At lunchtime, she spreads it to everyone in the deli. All these people would spread it to other people. Don't forget that tourist who was standing next to the woman on the subway. He is going back home tomorrow, and he is going to give it to the people on the plane, and so on. You can see what a disaster it would be.

If the disease did break out, there are two really big problems in stopping it. First, most doctors would not recognize the disease. They've never seen it in person, and unless they knew what to look for, it would be difficult to tell it apart from more routine cases. Second, there may not be enough of the vaccine stockpiled to cover everyone in the world.

Countries are becoming more prepared, though. After September 11, 2001, worry that a **bioterrorist** attack on U.S. soil would occur surfaced among health and governmental officials. Both the WHO and health agencies around the world came up with procedures to follow in case of attack. The WHO also created a Global Alert and Response (GAR) team, and has an advisory committee dedicated to smallpox eradication that meets every year. To inform the public, they posted smallpox awareness guidelines on their websites that are still updated today. This material details what you should do if the smallpox vaccine is released.

Smallpox is a serious disease that, if reintroduced to the world, could affect millions of people.

Other measures are being taken in the United States. In March 2013, the government purchased $463 million worth of a new smallpox medicine from a company called Siga Technologies. That amount is enough to make two million doses of the vaccine. But that is not the country's only stock. According to Dr. William H. Foege, a leader of the smallpox eradication effort, "If we had to, [the United States] could vaccinate the entire country in three days."

The Fate of Smallpox

The remaining known stocks of the smallpox virus were first scheduled to be destroyed in 1993, but their destruction has been delayed at each deadline since, including the most recent delay in May 2014.

Why the delay? People are torn on the issue. Some people do not want the disease destroyed entirely. They argue that if other countries (or even a terrorist group) have the disease, it's better we know everything we can about it so we can better deal with it, and they urge for more study. Likewise, a report by a group of scientists in *Science Daily* says that with today's advancements in **synthetic biology**, it could be possible to recreate "the live virus from scratch." If put into the wrong hands, however, it could annihilate large populations of the world.

If we could be sure all remaining traces of the live virus were in one or two places, eliminating it completely would seem like a natural and easy decision. It would be a step in the direction that Jenner had envisioned, to eliminate the "dreadful scourge of the human species" for good so that the virus could not harm anyone ever again. However, with remaining quantities unknown, and research goals unmet, it may be some time before we can say that the world is 100 percent smallpox-free.

Glossary

antibodies Cells in the body that attack and kill invaders.

bioterrorist A person who uses biological weapons to attack people or places.

compulsory Required by law.

eradicate To eliminate or destroy something.

domesticate To train an animal to need and accept the care of human beings.

host The living thing in which a virus lives.

inoculation The practice of taking a mild form of a disease and deliberately infecting a person with it to cause immunity to the disease.

membrane A thin sheet or layer of tissue that is part of a plant or an animal's body.

mercenary A soldier who will fight for any group or country that hires him.

Glossary

pustule A growth on the skin that fills with pus before turning into a scab.

quarantine To keep (a person or animal) away from others to prevent a disease from spreading.

sensitizes To cause (someone) to become sensitive to a substance and to react to it in a bad way.

surveillance-containment strategy The process used in the 1960s and 1970s to alert authorities of smallpox outbreaks. After hearing of an outbreak, health officials would rush to the community and immunize everyone.

synthetic biology The design of new biological parts or devices, or the redesign of already existing biological parts.

vaccination The practice of using a vaccine.

vaccine Name given by Edward Jenner to the matter taken from cowpox blisters and introduced into humans to provoke immunity to smallpox. Now refers to any substance given to provoke an immune response in humans, e.g., a flu vaccine.

variola major/minor Medical names for the two types of smallpox.

virus A microscopic organism that causes infection and can live only within the cells of a host.

white blood cells A cell in the blood that protects the body from disease.

World Health Organization (WHO) The body that oversees and manages world health practices and guidelines for the United Nations system.

For More Information

Interested in learning more about smallpox? Check out these websites and organizations.

Websites

Get Vaccinated!
www.nyhistory.org/exhibitions/smallpox
This is a companion site based on a 2012 exhibition organized by the New York Historical Society.

World Health Organization
www.who.int/topics/smallpox/en/
This official website gives facts about smallpox and explains what steps governments are taking in case of another outbreak.

Organizations

Centers for Disease Control and Prevention (CDC)
1600 Clifton Road
Atlanta, GA 30333
(404) 639-3311; (800) 232-4636
Website: www.cdc.gov

The Pan American Health Organization
Regional Office of the World Health Organization
525 Twenty-third Street NW
Washington, DC 20037
(202) 974-3000
Website: www.paho.org

For Further Reading

Gupta, Sunetra. *Pandemics: Our Fears and the Facts.* Seattle, WA: Amazon. Kindle Edition, 2013.

Henderson, D. A. and Richard Preston. *Smallpox: The Death of a Disease.* Amherst, NY: Prometheus Books, 2009.

Quammen, David. *Spillover: Animal Infections and the Next Human Pandemic.* New York, NY: W.W. Norton & Company, 2013.

Williams, Tony. *The Pox and the Covenant.* Naperville, IL: Sourcebooks, 2010.

Willrich, Michael. *Pox: An American History.* New York, NY: Penguin, 2012.

Index

Index